SCHIRMER'S LIBRARY
OF MUSICAL CLASSICS

Vol. 376

Muzio Clementi

Preludes and Exercises

School of Scales
In All the Major and Minor Keys
For Piano

Edited and Fingered by
MAX VOGRICH

ISBN 0-7935-1667-6

G. SCHIRMER, Inc.

DISTRIBUTED BY
HAL•LEONARD®
CORPORATION
7777 W. BLUEMOUND RD. P.O. BOX 13819 MILWAUKEE, WI 53213

Preludes and Exercises
School of Scales

Revised and fingered by
MAX VOGRICH

C major

M. CLEMENTI

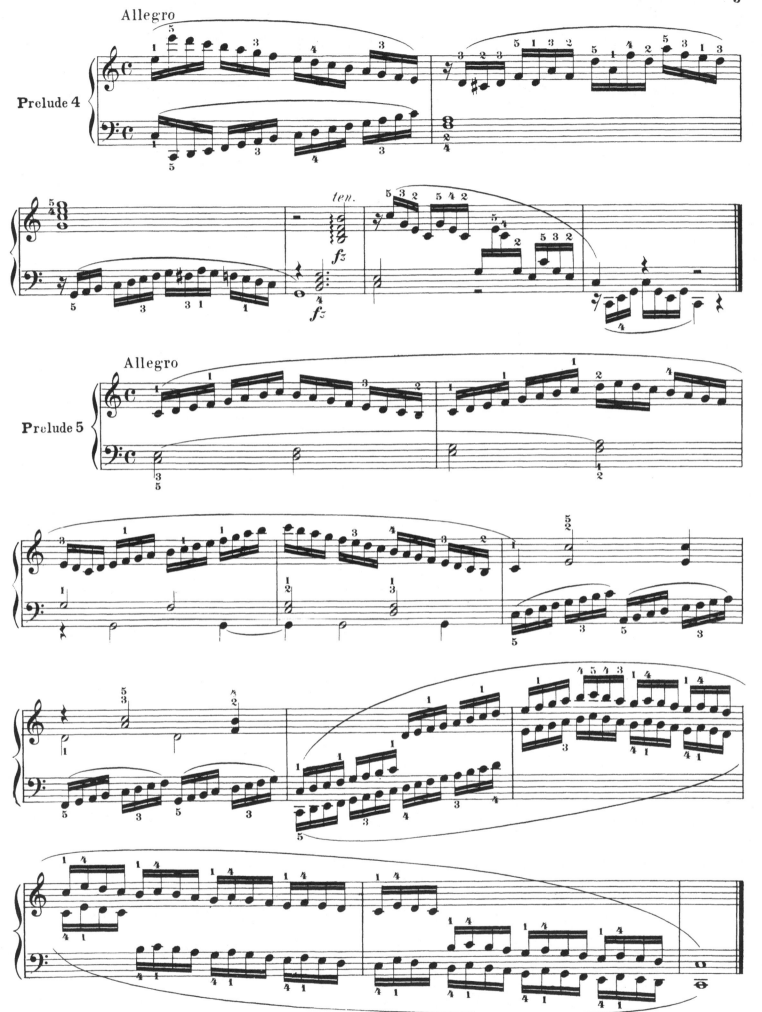

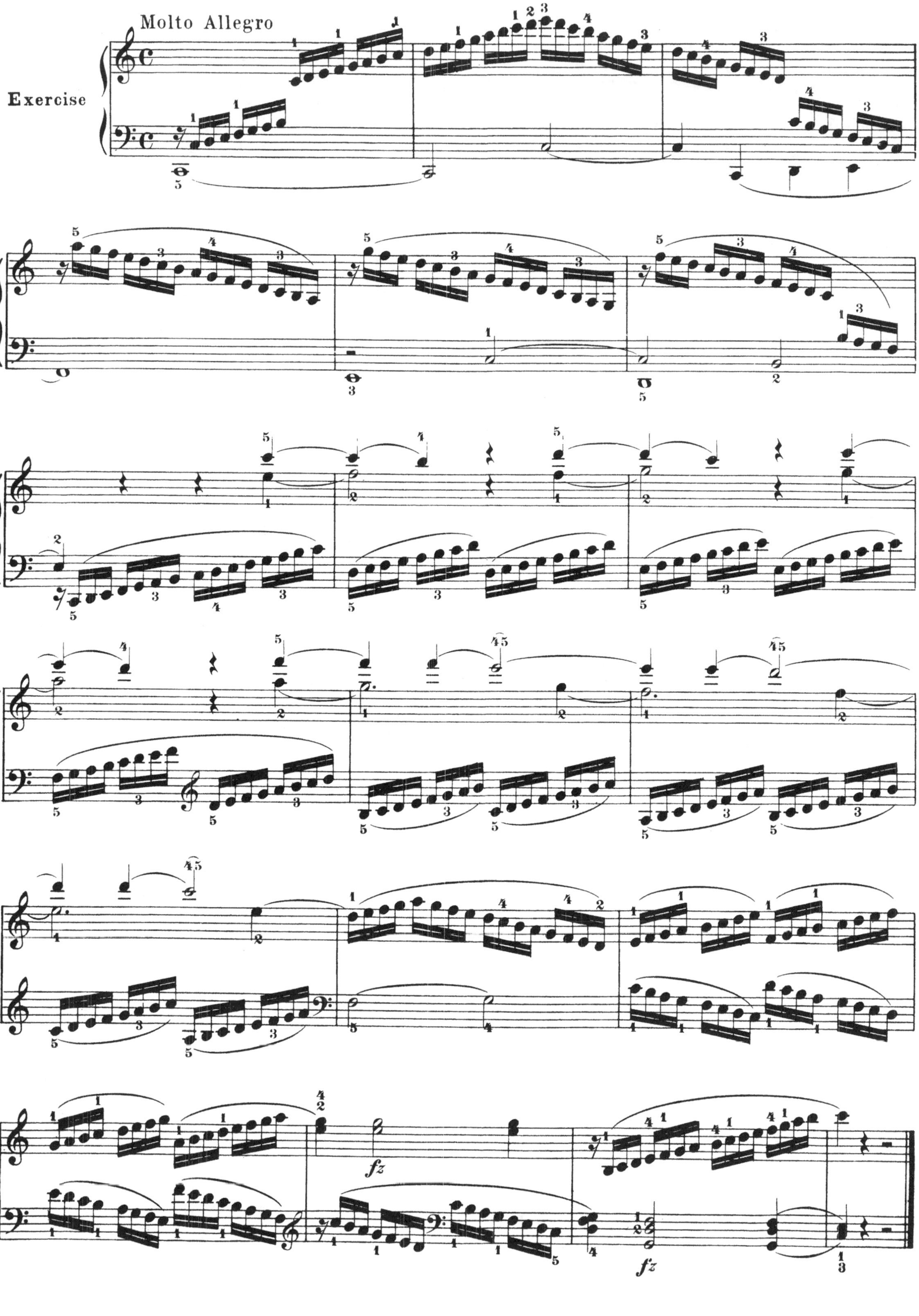
Molto Allegro
Exercise
fz
fz

A minor

Prelude

Exercise Allegro

F major

Prelude 1 · Allegro

Prelude 2 · Allegro

D minor

Prelude

sempre legato

10

Exercise

G major

Prelude 1

Moderato

Prelude 2

14

Allegrissimo

Exercise

legatissimo

E minor

Prelude

16

Allegro moderato

Exercise

*) Thumb over (not under.)

*) Thumb over.

B♭ major

Prelude

Exercise

Allegro

G minor

D major

Da capo al segno

Da capo al segno

B minor

Moderato

Prelude

Moderato

Exercise

E♭ major

Prelude

Exercise

C minor

Prelude

Moderato

legato

Exercise

Canone perpetuo
Allegro

A major

Prelude

Exercise Allegro

F♯ minor

A♭ major

Prelude · Moderato e legato

Exercise · Allegro moderato, ma con energia

F minor

E major

C♯ minor

42

D♭ major

Canone infinito
Allegro, ma non troppo

Exercise

B♭ minor

B major

Canone perpetuo

Exercise

48

G♯ minor

Canone infinito (in moto contrario)
Moderato

Exercise

F♯ major

Canone infinito (in moto contrario)
Allegro, ma non troppo

Exercise

E♭ minor

Grand Exercise
in all the Major and Minor Keys

G# minor

E major

C# minor

64

stacc.

pp

f

A major

64

C major